A SPACE IMAGINED

A SPACE IMAGINED

by *POWilson*

The Arts Forum, NYC

taf
NYC

The Arts Forum, NYC
Brooklyn, New York
www.theartsforum.com

The following poems, by the author, also appear in his book, "On
the Side of a Fish": believe, beyond, leave open, it is a weight,
right in front of us, hands, I can see, two lizards and a fly, defiance,
reinvented, in a glance and stand here only.

Contents

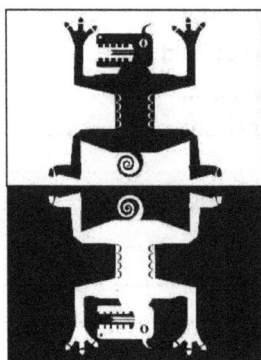

- *leave open*

open a hand and let fall
all that once was desire
all kept here is cumbersome
and worse, all kept hidden
cancer

the perfected noon sun
has no shadow,
the perfectly shot arrow
no ark, and these things too
are dreams, painted
by desire, kept

open a hand and let fall
all that once was left
from things once thrown away

give victory and romance to fantasy
take now only those things
that do not need
a hand or a thought
to hold them

- *silence loud*

there are times
the silence talks so loud
it is deafening

it says, what is here
that is not magic

we confuse familiar with understood
known as less than amazing

the world is born fresh
with the gaze of every child,
every person new
with a childlike gaze

we have been hypnotized
by a barrage of spectacular events,
as something in the solar wind
seems to try to break the spell

- *drowning of thirst*

we open our eyes to a desert or a storm
and who has ever been given to choose

yet this is the reference by which we judge all things

whether we fear drowning or dying of thirst

whether we love to think of endings
or lovingly speak of birth

- *where were you when you heard*

where were you when you heard?
and lips reply
not trees, grass, red water
ancient bearded faces, robes and stone
not these
but a hand painted photograph
of a too clean family,
short parted hair
combed and pasted,
smiling white through the glare

where were you when you heard?
memory echoes
and eyes reply;
not sheep, chariots, sandals,
ancient bearded faces, robes and stone,
but these;
a cartoon animal skipping
as a garbage truck wails
like an elephant in the street,
sprayed words on a burnt brick wall
and a magazine on a coffee table

- *this thing inside*

once, then
these things enchanted me
these living things
this thing inside
these living things

and moments when I am still
while the world is still moving
I feel it here, this thing
that does not move but causes motion
this thing-less thing you say has left
I have left it too
it does not leave

so then we call no use
bring me this mysterious
so I can judge this thing exists
and will not see
this thing inside
I have hidden too
it does not hide

- *come to me clearly*

come to me clearly
these faint suggestions
I cannot know as other than self,
and I am alone

and if it is only a maker
to what was made
then I am still alone

come to me clearly
these rainbows of hope only appear
when the weather is just so,
like the mood of poetry –
trashed by the noise of the day

\

- sometimes we leave

sometimes we leave
things, people, times
like surgery, we remove ourselves
from a Siamese twin who wanted us to go
demanded we stay
and left us to choose

sometimes,
when we are lost,
and have finally lost enough,
with water left on the stove boiling,
and unsorted papers on a file cabinet

sometimes we leave without ceremony
quietly, unnoticed,
as leaves fall
and car noises fade

an old man sits on a sign painted bench,
a dog bark is heard from a half mile away
and something in the quietness
says go

- all to now

all that we have done to now;
time stolen,
words cheated,
promise unfulfilled
love unrequited,
chances not taken,
memories missed,
stones thrown returned and not returned,
sweat gone vapor,
yours given is mine,
mine given is to me gone,
and all to now is even

- *we move backwards*

we move backwards towards birth,
before we were in the womb
we imagine, we knew everything
something says remember
don't leave, and we run,
life, death and wanting
pulling us away

we move backwards towards birth,
every age the new age stirred
by the supposed futility of the last,
all of us peasants in royal clothes,
all of us royal in peasant housing,
disbelieving we are known

we move backwards towards birth,
church bells ringing, beautiful
five miles away among trees,
softened by a light wind,
not heard if only heard

we are not deaf to sounding drums,
our own hearts beating,
bells pounding,
only softened by space,
we move backwards
towards birth,
hoping to shed these royal clothes
and peasant homes

- *your hands can not hold me*

your hands can not hold me
but one word has
I don't know souls or time,
begin, end, or eternity,
I just know children playing
and that is too much to know
too little to know answers,
each moment almost,
or not at all,
here as the eyelid closes
gone as it reopens

- *stand here only*

stand here only
and let it come in,
there is no need to close
what cannot help but closing

a life lived simply, purely
without pretense,
human
as a tree is a tree,
one transient moment of beauty

I want only
to sing in the night sky
the melody
the sky is singing
perfectly hollow
cool breeze, and open

- *the dream door closes*

the dream door closes
and you can't get in,
a moment ago
I ran freely with things
that others could only wish,
now,
I stand naked in the hall

- *the third horizon*

a snow covered hill flowing into other hills
strung together by a black lace tree line
against a terra cotta sunrise,
and from there
the grey blue sky goes on,
like water floating over fire

this is the second horizon,
like the edge of a universe,
and the third is unseen
beyond a minds reach

- *this speck of will*

this speck of will,
invisible seed,
wisp of hope,
unspeakable essence

that remains
when everything else
is stripped away
is all I claim,

everything else
it seems to me –
is rented

- tender these words

tender these words and charms,
pretend this chase if you do not know
and tender all,
talk whispers if others are heard
only melody, not words,
paint with colors if you must
but leave only gray to be cut and placed
into this tendering vase,
walk invisibly through bones–

walk softly across this floor
and even more softly through these halls,
be little more than wind when entering rooms,
the broken glass you see is mine,
left there once in the darkness
for the one who sang soprano,
or played the flute,
or did not sing at all,
left in years waiting
for someone who might have known,
or at least suspected –
a giant is sleeping

- believe

on hands and knees
counting these blades of grass
imagining there is no sky,
no vastness,
or raindrops to feed the grass,
and the grass says only
believe

- beyond

as a child we look up at the night sky
and see the stars
and imagine the space around them,
and how far it goes on

then this question comes
of where it stops, and if it stops
then what is beyond that?
and then beyond

then here, at this moment
like a great swelling hollow
an awareness comes;
that a self is contained
in a very small body,
and imagination reaches outside of it,
beyond sight
and knowledge

then humility,
then awe,
and this unquenchable idea
that there is something more to existing
than what is known...
and within this sense of wonder,
our only evidence

- *defiance*

these melodies come pleading,
joyful sorrowfulness
with children's lyric,
this simple tune given
like a toy,
always returned
barely breathing,
falling back
then up through conflict,
still singing
though outside of joy,
singing only
in defiance

- in a reflection

is that you I remember or myself?
are those your eyes or mine?
clear as water, opaque enough to see
yet transparent enough to see through

my reflection still but dancing,
more bearable translucent,
less mortal, less confined

we see our own reflection and dream
we are reflection, not caged by time

then we rage like troubled water
and nothing is reflected,
with only these moments
when words escape us,
and for a moment a reflection,
just before the water is stirred

- *it is a weight*

it is a weight
so we throw it down
this livingness is in the way of living,
this felt-ness that gives cause to live
is cumbersome and in the way of striving
so we cast it away and lose all cause for striving,
we try so hard to give out only
and even the slightest joy
proves too heavy

- *a space imagined*

I held each thing to be everything, all
and left
broken

this place not filled
takes things in but cannot hold them

those things, other, away
that could not stay
their promise like a stone falling
in a gesture to a phrase

loving flees
to an empty room
still not ready to confess;
the realization of a dream
is the end of a dream

space is nothing some have said
but when I need room
I imagine it, first
inside my head
then larger in steps
until it takes all in
there is no need to hold anything
in a space imagined

everything imaginable,
is within

- *I can see*

I can see through all this madness
to a place of floating calm
out beyond the reptiles unchecked hunger
turning, turning land of awe